JOSEPH

DESTINED TO RULE

A Study In Integrity And Divine Affirmation

by Dr. J. Robert Clinton

JOSEPH
DESTINED TO RULE

JOSEPH
DESTINED TO RULE

A SENSE OF DESTINY

But He sent a man ahead of them,
Joseph, who had been sold as a slave.
His feet were kept in chains,
And an iron collar was around his neck,
Until what he had predicted came true.
The word of the Lord tested him.
Psa 105:17-19

JOSEPH
DESTINED TO RULE

Preface

Leadership development is a life-time process in which God interacts in the life of a leader to point out potential for leadership, develop that potential in the leader, guide that leader into service, and use that leader for His own purposes.

A leader may be born with potential to lead but it is God who shapes that leader so that the potential is realized. Opportunities, experience, and training (formal, non-formal, informal) all combine with giftedness to make a leader. And God is active in the whole process.

The major events, people, circumstances, crises, etc. through which God works to develop and guide and use a leader are called process items. The whole idea of leadership development and process items are described fully in my self study text called *Leadership Emergence Theory*. Definitions of process items from that book which apply to this study are included in an appendix at the end of this study. The *Leadership Emergence Theory* book is available through Barnabas Publishers.

Joseph is a particularly good Bible character to study since his life illustrates many of the concepts of leadership emergence theory.

I. Summary Sheet

Person Studied: Joseph (son of Jacob)

Direct Data: See Appendix A. List of Vignettes

Indirect Data: Psa 105:16-25

Acts 7:9-15

Heb 11:22

I Chron 5:2

Josh 24:32

Abbreviated Time-line

I. Seeds of Destiny	II. Blessed Buffeting		III. Destiny Fulfilled			
Vignettes 1-4	A. Potiphar Vig 6,7	B. Jailer Vig 8,9	A. Pre-famine Vig 12	B. Famine Vig 13-15	C. Deliverance Vig 17-19	D. Celebration Vig 19-25
	Vig 5 Sold into Slavery		Vig 10,11 into Pharaoh's Service		Vig 16 Jacob's Vision at Beersheba	
Age	17		30			105

GIFT-MIX: Revelatory Gifts (wisdom, interpretation of dreams)

SPHERE OF INFLUENCE: Nation wide - Egypt

MAJOR CONTRIBUTIONS:

1. Joseph adds to our knowledge of the divine affirmation process item.

2. Joseph adds to our understanding of the word check process item specifically and revelatory gifts in general.

3. Joseph highlights integrity as a key quality of leadership which God affirms.

4. Joseph is probably the classical study of a sense of destiny.

5. Joseph highlights in seed form the major essentials of leadership.

II. Joseph - Motivation/Expectations For The Study

Long Time Interest

A Bible teacher, I can't remember who now, at a local church Bible conference made an introductory statement which caught my attention and has stayed with me. "There are three characters in the Bible for which the Bible does not say anything negative — Joseph, Daniel and Jesus." Now whether that is actually true or not is a matter all its own. However, it served to interest me in Joseph and Daniel as Old Testament characters worthy of special note. I have done a formal study on Daniel. I've done partial studies on Joseph. I've personally long wanted to study Joseph in more detail. Now it's time for me to do something about that desire.

In my pre-thoughts about Joseph I anticipate that I am going:

1. To see the "left-hand of God"[1] at work and to note the process items which correlate with that providential working (Gen 45:5,7; 50:2; Psa 105:17; Acts 7:9,10),

2. To study the concept "sense of destiny" and identify essential elements of that concept as reflected in Joseph's life,

3. To reflect on the generalized time-line phases to see how Joseph's unique time-line reflects these generalized phases,

4. To expand my understanding of several major process items, among which are: word check, sovereign guidance (double confirmation), sense of destiny, etc.,

5. To identify in seed form some essentials of leadership,

6. To list some observations concerning leadership principles.

---

1 Dr. Arthur Glasser (Fuller School of World Mission) describes the behind-the-scenes providential working of God utilizing people not in the direct redemptive line (Right Hand of God) as the "left hand of God."

If I can make even a small measure of progress on these items, I will be satisfied.

In addition, two major reasons for doing this study include,

1. Having a model Biblical study that I can point to regarding format, method of display, etc.

2. Having a ready source of material on a Biblical character from which I can teach and illustrate leadership emergence concepts when I'm in workshops, seminars, conferences and other field situations which require a "popularized communication" format to carry important theoretical ideas.

III. Joseph Capsule

Development Phase I. Seeds of Destiny

A Child Of Rachel -Whom Jacob Loved

Joseph was the first child born to Jacob and Rachel and the 12th[2] to Jacob. His birth occurred in Mesopotamia while Jacob was still working for Laban. It is of significance that he is the firstborn of Rachel who only of Jacob's wives and concubines is described as "the one he loved."[3] Jacob was old when Joseph was born (most likely 91). So Joseph was special to him on two accounts - Rachel's firstborn and a child born later in Jacob's life. That he was special to Jacob is highlighted by the "coat of many colors,"[4] which caused his 10 older brothers to be jealous of him.

A Child Given In Answer To Prayer

The name Joseph was given to him by his mother Rachel at his birth. Apparently, it had a two-fold significance.[5] It signified that God had answered Rachel's prayers for a child and taken away her reproach at being childless. It also prophetically signaled

---

[2] That Joseph is 12th assumes that Dinah was born before Joseph.

[3] See Gen 29:18, 20, 30, 31, 32, 33.

[4] The "coat of many colors" (KJV) is translated as "a long robe with full sleeves" in modern versions. M.G. Kyle (*International Standard Bible Encyclopedia*), p. 1738, suggests customs of the times indicate that just such kinds of coats were used to indicate royalty or rulership. He sees the possibility of the coat being ceremonial - that is, a token of rank. In a rhetorical question, Kyle implies that Jacob indicated, by the coat, his intention to give Joseph the precedence and the succession as chieftain of the tribe. He states that it is difficult otherwise to account for the insane jealousy of the older brethren (Gen 37:4).

[5] See Gen 30:22-24 where Rachel names Joseph at his birth. It is clear to her mind that Joseph was an answer to prayer. God took away her reproach. Also, she saw that she would yet have another child. The Good News Bible has a footnote which indicates this two-fold significance of the name. That footnote (*Good News Bible*, p. 31) indicates that Joseph sounds like the Hebrew for "may he give another" and "he has taken away." It is significant to see that God's timing is involved in this, that Rachel had prayed, and that Joseph was born at the time of God's choosing.

to Rachel that God would give her another child in the future. It is significant that Joseph was given in answer to prayer. Rachel had not been able to bear a child for 9 or 10 years. She had taken this burden to the Lord. And he answered in his timing.

Family Conflict

Joseph grew up in a family situation which involved intense rivalry. There were two "official" wives and their children and there were two "unofficial" wives and their children. Leah, the older wife whom Jacob had been tricked into marrying,[6] had five sons and a daughter. Three of these, Reuben, Simeon, and Levi were born early in Jacob and Leah's marriage. These boys were in their late teens and early twenties when Joseph was born. Leah's other two sons, Issachar and Zebulun, were probably under 10 years of age at the time of Joseph's birth. Leah's daughter, Dinah, was born very nearly at the same time as Joseph. Leah's handmaiden, Zilphah had two sons, Gad and Asher, who were probably almost teenagers at Joseph's birth. Rachel's handmaiden, Bilhah had two sons, Dan and Naphtali, who were most likely in their middle teens at Joseph's birth. Each of the wives and two concubines, of course, would seek to do the best for her children. That there was intense rivalry can be seen in the mandrake incident between Leah and Rachel.[7] The bargain showed that Rachel had the most influence with Jacob and that there was bitterness between Leah and Rachel. The two concubines, Bilhah and Zilphah, would have even less influence with Jacob and would seek any means to insure that their sons would not be left out of Jacob's favor or inheritance. It was into this situation that Joseph

---

6 See Genesis 29:21-27.

7 The mandrake incident in Gen 30:14-16 shows at least two major things. 1) Rachel had the most influence with Jacob. Apparently, she was in such control of Jacob that he was not having any physical relationship with Leah at this time. 2) Rachel was desperate to have a child. The mandrakes were plants which were used to increase fertility. Whether these plants worked or not, we do not know. We do know that Rachel did become pregnant and accredited it to answered prayer from God.

would grow up - wives who were in rivalry for Jacob's attention and favor for their children.

Conflict And Crises - God's Hand

Joseph grew up knowing about and seeing his Uncle Laban's devious dealings[8] with Jacob. In turn, he saw Jacob's methods of tricking Laban[9] and obtaining wealth (flocks). He saw Jacob's flight from Laban. He saw the encounter with Laban after Laban caught up with the caravan.[10] He saw the search for Laban's household gods (which his own mother had stolen).[11] He saw the memorial[12] between Jacob and Laban and knew of God's sovereign interference[13] which kept Laban from attacking Jacob. He saw the crisis concerning the meeting with Esau. He saw how his father prepared to meet Esau - the presents sent ahead and the ordering of the families and material goods.[14] The line up of goods and families that would meet Esau gives an indication of the priority[15] in relationship to Jacob. He knew of his father's

---

8 Laban tricked Jacob in regards to his marriage with Rachel. He consistently used him to manage his flocks without giving fair pay. See Gen 30:25-43. See also Gen 31:7, 41.

9 See Gen 30:37-43 especially for Jacob's "devious" methods. Verse 39 indicates some kind of "sympathetic magic."

10 See Gen 31:22-42. This was a serious encounter. Laban could have easily taken revenge on Jacob and killed him and his families. Verse 27 does highlight Jacob's deviousness (at least in Laban's eyes).

11 See Gen 31:33-35. This incident shows that deceit was part of the actions of Rachel as well as Laban and Jacob. Other indications, Reuben (Gen 38), Simeon and Levi (Gen 34:25-29), the brothers' lying to Jacob when they sold Joseph, etc. show that lying and deception were part of the world view of the whole family. This makes Joseph's integrity stand out even more.

12 See Gen 31:43-55.

13 See Gen 31:29. Joseph knew also that God was with Jacob (see Gen 30:27).

14 This was crisis. Perhaps Esau was coming out to kill Jacob. Perhaps the gifts did pacify him. It is clear that Jacob didn't want to stay around too long in Esau's presence.

15 See Gen 33:2.

wrestling with God[16] and his new name. He thus experienced the deliverance of his family from two major crises by the living God of his father Jacob. The shift from Mesopotamia to Canaan was a major event in Joseph's life. It signals the end of the first sub-phase of Joseph's foundational development phase.

Family Crisis

Joseph's brothers hated him intensely. There are at least three reasons for this. One, Joseph was apparently singled out as having Jacob's love (see Gen 37:3). Because he was so loved, Joseph, although motherless, apparently had the ear of Jacob. Joseph "brought bad reports"[17] concerning what his brothers did. Two, the "coat" probably did indicate that Jacob had already picked Joseph to be his direct successor. Three, Joseph's dreams which placed him as ruler over them infuriated them further. In any case, the brothers (most likely Dan, Naphtali, Gad and Asher were the ringleaders) decided to get rid of Joseph.

One day when Jacob sent Joseph to see how the brothers and the flocks were doing. The brothers saw Joseph at a distance and plotted to kill him. Reuben tried to save Joseph's life and suggested that they throw him in a pit. Notice that the brothers ripped off the "coat" probably indicating that it was more than just a "coat" (see Gen 37:23). At that time (providentially), a caravan appeared that was bound for Egypt. Judah talked the brothers into selling Joseph to the caravan. Notice that it was Leah's sons (Reuben and Judah) who tried to help Joseph. This crisis event closes Joseph's foundational development phase.

---

16 See Gen 32:22-32. It is significant that this sense of destiny experience just precedes Jacob's actual face to face meeting with Esau.

17 Notice that it is the sons of Bilhah (Dan, Naphtali) and Zilpah (Gad, Asher). These sons would have the least favor with Jacob since they were not sons of the two wives. They were also nearer in age to Joseph than Leah's older sons.

Development Phase 2. Blessed Buffeting

Sold Into Potiphar's Household

Joseph was sold into an upper class home. Potiphar, an Egyptian and the Captain of the Palace Guard, became the owner of Joseph. Joseph prospered. His master perceived that the Lord was with Joseph and brought success to whatever he did.[18] So Potiphar made Joseph his personal servant. Then he put Joseph in charge of the household. In each ministry task given him, Joseph did it well. Potiphar then turned over everything he had unto Joseph.

Integrity Check[19]

Potiphar's wife tempted Joseph repeatedly to have sexual intercourse. He steadfastly refused. Joseph saw that if he gave in to the temptation he would be sinning against God. His inner integrity would not let him do this. Potiphar's wife after one specific refusal accused Joseph of raping her. Potiphar had Joseph arrested and put into prison.[20]

A Further Outward Setback - Jail

Joseph quickly gained the approval of the jailer and before long he was made responsible for everything that was done in

---

18 See Gen 39:2,3,5. This concept of divine affirmation (approval and accompanying success to Joseph) stand out in the life of Joseph. His evident submission to God in each situation (Jas 4:10) was rewarded by God's further use of Joseph and exaltation of him.

19 Integrity check is the name in leadership emergence theory given to the process item which God uses to confirm inner character. Usually the successful passing of an integrity check results in affirmation by God usually in the expansion of one's sphere of influence.

20 Kyle (I.S.B.E. P. 1739) indicates that the fact that Potiphar didn't immediately put Joseph to death is very significant. Most likely it indicates that Potiphar didn't believe his wife's accusations but, for the sake of appearances, had Joseph put into prison.

prison. Again, the Scriptures confirm that it was "because the Lord was with him."[21]

Divine Contact

Joseph was in prison for some time. During this time, two of the King's special servants were put into prison. One was a wine steward and the other was the chief baker. Apparently, they had offended the King. These two men each had a dream on the same night. Joseph[22] was able to interpret both of the dreams. Both of the dreams came true just as Joseph had predicted. The chief baker was put to death but the wine steward was restored to his original position. Joseph told his story of innocence to the wine steward, including his kidnaping and the incident with Potiphar's wife. He asked the wine steward to remember him to the King. The wine steward immediately forgot Joseph but later would be God's link to move Joseph into prominence.

The King's Two Dreams

Some two years later, the King of Egypt had two different dreams which upset him. None of his wise men nor magicians could interpret the dreams. The wine steward remembered the prison incident. He told the King how Joseph had interpreted both his own dream and that of the chief baker. The King sent for Joseph. Joseph[23] indicated that the dreams were from God. The two dreams were a form of double confirmation. He then interpreted the dreams as indicating that there would be seven years in which the harvests would be plentiful followed by seven

---

21 See Gen 39:19,23 where it is clear that Joseph had God's divine approval. God was superintending each step of Joseph's development.

22 These dreams would provide the "divine contact" which would later be used to link Joseph to Pharaoh.

23 Notice in both the revelatory incidents (Gen 40:8 and Gen 41:16), Joseph claimed that it was God who gives the interpretation of dreams.

years of terrible famine. He then suggested a plan whereby grain could be stored during the seven years of plenty. His plan was accepted as good wisdom. In fact, Pharaoh appointed Joseph to oversee the whole operation. Joseph was given a role in which his authority was second only to Pharaoh.

Development Phase 3. Destiny Fulfilled

A New Beginning In Egypt

Pharaoh gave Joseph an Egyptian name - Zaphenath. He also gave Joseph a wife, Asenath, the daughter of Potiphera, a priest in the city of Heliopolis. Two boys were born to him, Manasseh[24] and Ephraim.[25]

Joseph began his duties as minister of economic affairs at age thirty. He traveled widely in this job and soon knew the whole country. His plan of taking 20% of the crops as taxes was implemented. During the seven years of plenty much grain was stored up for the troublesome times to come.

Famine Widespread

The famine was much wider spread than just Egypt. It affected Canaan where Joseph's family was. Jacob learned that there was grain available in Egypt. He sent the ten older brothers (Benjamin stayed home) to buy grain and to bring it back to Canaan.

Joseph's Boyhood Dream Comes True

Joseph's brothers came to Egypt to buy grain. Joseph was selling grain to people from all over the world. When he saw his brothers, he recognized them but they did not recognize Joseph. He questioned them and tested them. They told the story of their family. He accused them of being spies and said he would keep one of them as hostages until they returned with their

---

[24] In Gen 41:51, we see some of the inner sufferings that Joseph had felt during the thirteen years he was working for Potiphar and in jail. God has made me forget all my sufferings and all my father's family. Manasseh was given a name which sounds like the Hebrew for "cause to forget", the major thrust of Gen 41:51 (see *Good News Bible* p. 45).

[25] Ephraim's name meaning "give children" captures the thrust of the meaning of Gen 41:52, "God has given me children in the land of my trouble."

younger brother. If they returned with their younger brother, he would accept their story as being true. He sent them on their way with full sacks of grain (and the money they had paid for the grain secretly put back in their sacks). Later, they found the money and were frightened at what it might mean.

The Famine Grows Worse - Second Trip Of Jacob's Sons

The famine worsened. Jacob had to send the brothers back a second time. They were frightened to go unless they met Joseph's condition to bring along Benjamin. After some difficult persuasion, in which Reuben offered to guarantee Benjamin's safety, Jacob sent them back with Benjamin.

Joseph still pretended not to know the brothers. After giving them the grain they wanted, he planned a special test for them. He placed his own silver cup in Benjamin's grain sack. After sending the brothers on their way, he sent his servant to stop them and search for the silver cup. When it was found in Benjamin's sack, the brothers were dismayed. Judah offered to be taken in place of Benjamin and thus demonstrated courage and integrity. He also confessed that it was God who was bringing judgment on the brothers. Joseph then admitted to the brothers who he really was.

The brothers were frightened that Joseph would take revenge but Joseph reveals his inner integrity and points out his discerning of God's work in the entire process.

Joseph Sends Word For The Whole Family To Come To Egypt

Joseph sent word to his father, Jacob, to bring the entire family to Egypt since the famine was to last another five years. Jacob received a word from God concerning the move to Egypt. The entire family went to Egypt.

Jacob's Last Words

Jacob, before dying, demanded of Joseph that his body be taken back and buried with his fathers. Joseph made a vow to do so. Jacob blessed Joseph's descendants with a prophetic blessing. He then gave his final words of blessings to his sons. After his death, Joseph honored his vow and took Jacob back and buried him in the cave at Machpelah, east of Mamre, in the field which Abraham had bought.

Joseph's Integrity, Faith/Wish, Destiny Fulfilled

After his father's death, Joseph's brothers feared Joseph would take revenge on them. But Joseph shows his integrity as well as his understanding of his destiny in God's plan. His last leadership act was to encourage his people to a future hope. He made them promise that when they went back to their own land that they would take his remains with them and bury him back in his own land. This tremendous act of faith was eventually fulfilled.[26]

---

26 See Joshua 24:32. Note also the reference to this act of faith in Hebrews 11:22.

IV. Overview Chart
Joseph's Leadership Emergence Processes - Overviewed

	I. Seeds of Destiny	II. Blessed Buffeting	III. Destiny-Fulfilled
	A. Conflict - Survival B. Early Crisis - Survival C. Divine Foreshadowing - Survival	A. Potiphar B. Jailer	A. Pre Famine B. Famine C. Deliverance D. Celebration
Age	17	30	105
Key People	• Jacob • Esau • Laban • Reuben • Rachel • Judah	• Potiphar • Wine steward • Potiphar's wife • Baker • Jailer • Pharaoh	• Pharaoh
Key Events	• divine protection (Gen 31:24) • solemn agreement (Gen 31:43-55) • Jacob meets Esau (Gen 33) • Shechem Massacre (Gen 34) • Rachel's Death (Gen 35) • Isaac's Death (Gen 35) • SOD - Dreams (Gen 37) • Sold Into Slavery (Gen 37)	• Temptation • Prisoner's Dreams • Pharaoh's Dreams	• Convergence • Faith/Act

Major Process Items	• Family - Conflict
	• Crises
	  Laban Pursues
	  Esau's Revenge
	  Shechem Massacre
	  Rachel's Death
	  Isaac's Death
	  Sold Into Slavery
	• Sense of Destiny
	  Birth/name
	  Peniel
	  Dreams
		• Divine Affermation
		• Integrity Check
		• Isolation
		• Word Check
		• Divine Contact
		• Sovereign Guidance
			• Word Check
			• Sense of Destiny
			• Integrity Check
			• Divine Affirmation

Role/
Sphere of Influence
	family member
	leading heir
		• personal servant
		• household steward
		• steward of all of Potiphar's
		  holdings
		• Steward of Jailer's affairs
			• Minister of Economics/Production
			  for all of Egypt

V. Detailed Chart Phase I: Seeds of Destiny
Joseph's Life: Phase 1. Seeds of Destiny - Survival

	A. CONFLICT SURVIVAL	B. EARLY CRISIS SURVIVAL	C. DIVINE FORESHADOWING SURVIVAL
Location	Mesopotamia	Canaan	Canaan
Age	0 3, 4	5,6	17
Boundary	Laban Crisis	Rachel's Death	Sold Into Slavery
Data	Gen 31:22-31:55 Gen 32-34	Gen 35:16-20	Gen 37:12-36

Major Process Items	• Family - Conflict
	  - Laban/Jacob
	  - wives/concubines
	• Family - SOD
	  -Birth/mom's prayer
	  - name/given by mom
		• Crisis - Laban
		  - sovereign protection at
		  Gilead
		• Peniel - SOD
		• Crisis - Esau
		• Crisis - Shechem
		  Massacre (rape of Dinah)
			• Crisis - Isaac's Death
			• Family - conflict/brother's
			• Sovereign Guidance
			  sense of destiny
			• Sovereign Guidance
			  double confirmation
			• Crisis - sold into slavery

Significant Person/ Event	• Jacob
	• Laban
	
	• divine protection
	  (Gen 31:24,29)
	• solemn agreement
		• Rachel
		• Esau
		
		• Jacob meets Esau
		  (Gen 33)
		• Shechem massacre
		  (Gen 34)
		• Rachel dies (Gen 35)
			• Jacob
			• Reuben
			• Judah
			• Isaac's death (Gen 35)
			• SOD - dreams (Gen 37)
			• sold into slavery (Gen 37)

A. Narrative Explanation Of Phase I.
Seeds Of Destiny - Survival

Overview

This development phase covers Joseph's life from birth until 17 years of age. It has 3 sub-phases, each marked with a crisis boundary condition: the Laban Crisis, the Rachel Crisis and the Slavery Crisis. In each of these, Joseph learned providential survival lessons. Family process items (many involving conflict), crises process items and sense of destiny items highlight this foundational phase. The end result of this was a young person:

- who sensed the presence of God in his life,
- who was already evincing integrity,
- who had experienced God's protective hand in crises and survived them.

Sub-Phase A: Conflict - Survival

The major process items for this phase include:

1. Family - Conflict (sibling rivalry, co-wife rivalry, family atmosphere of deceit, jealousy, etc.)
2. Family - Sense of Destiny (birth and name giving)
3. Family - Crisis (Laban confrontation)

Process Item 1. Family - Conflict

Appendix B shows Jacob's children by Leah and Zilpah and by Rachel and Bilhah. Jealousy, deceit and vying for Jacob's attention were all a part of the scene in which Joseph grew up. Joseph's mother, Rachel, was Jacob's favorite wife. Joseph being the 12th of 13 children (meaning he arrived later in Jacob's life and being Rachel's long-awaited first-born) made Joseph the favorite child of Jacob. This served to increase the conflict of Joseph's home life. The amazing thing is that out of this family influence, which certainly was not conducive to integrity, came a person of such integrity.

Process Item 2. Family - Sense Of Destiny

Joseph was given in answer to Rachel's prayer.[27] It is clear from the narrative that God dealt with Rachel concerning her attitude toward Leah (and Jacob's attitude, too).[28] The Genesis account reckons Rachel's barrenness as God's doing. So that, at least three things should be noted:

1. Joseph was given in answer to Rachel's prayers.

2. The timing of Joseph's birth was God's timing - He could have given Joseph at any time during the first 15 years or so in which Rachel was barren.

3. Joseph's name was a significant reminder of God's intervention. It was a memorial to God's deliverance on Rachel's behalf.[29]

As a young lad, Joseph was probably reminded over and over by his mother that he was special. He was an answer to prayer. God's hand was upon his life.

Process Item 3. Family Crisis (God's Intervention)

The boundary event for sub-phase 1 was the major confrontation[30] between Laban and Jacob. This occurred after Jacob had stolen away with his wives, children, cattle and Laban's

---

27 See Gen 30:22.

28 See Gen 29:31,33; 30:1,8 et al, that point out that there was disharmony and jealousy with the polygamous family life and that Rachel had a poor attitude toward Leah.

29 See footnote 5 which cites the *Good News Bible's* interpretation of this name.

30 The confrontation had been building for some time. Notice Gen 31:1,2. Laban's sons felt Jacob was tricking Laban and would deplete Laban's flocks eventually. Laban, himself had changed in attitude toward Jacob. Jacob talks over the problem with Rachel and Leah. In his conversation, we learn that God's sovereignly brought about this confrontation for it was God who, in a dream, told Jacob what to do concerning the flocks.

household gods.[31] God set up the crisis and then clearly delivered in the crisis.[32] This deliverance in a crisis situation would have made deep impression on a young lad of Joseph's age. Most likely, he would be reminded of the major times in the life of Abraham, Isaac and Jacob when God had intervened in the past. A sense of a God-given heritage became part of Joseph's background.

Sub-Phase B. Early Crises - Survival

A series of major crises mark sub-phase B. The boundary condition just described above was followed by:

- the Esau crisis,
- the Shechem Massacre crisis,
- the crisis involved with Rachel's death.

Preceding the Esau crisis, God met Jacob at Peniel in a landmark sense of destiny experience. In all of these experiences, survival was seen to be intertwined with God's sovereign working. The loss of Rachel, at an early age, must have been devastating to Joseph. Joseph was most likely drawn closer to Jacob. Without direct data, we can only surmise that Joseph early-on learned that life was to be full of crises but that God could providentially work through them for His purposes.

---

31 The *Scofield Bible* footnotes Gen 31:30 concerning why Laban was so greatly concerned about the household gods that Rachel had stolen (31:19). It points out that archaeological investigations have shown that in northern Mesopotamia that possession of the household gods of a father-in-law by a son-in-law was legally acceptable as proof of the designation of that son-in-law as a principle heir. This would account why Laban was so upset and went to great trouble to follow Jacob. It would also explain why Jacob got so angry (Gen 31:36).

32 Verses 31:7,9,10-13 indicate that God was behind the confrontation and was getting ready to take Jacob back to the land of his birth. Verse 31:29 shows that God clearly was delivering in the incident.

Sub-Phase C. Divine Foreshadowing - Survival

Major process items include:

1. Crisis - Isaac's death
2. Family - conflict (brothers/integrity)
3. Sense of destiny (sovereign guidance, double confirmation, prophetic, word check)
4. Crises - conflict, sold into slavery, isolation, geographic relocation

Process Item 1. Crisis - Isaac's Death

His grandfather's death would serve to remind him of the Godly heritage of which he was a part.

Process Item 2. Family Conflict (brothers/integrity)

As Joseph moved into his teen-age years, the jealousy of his half-brothers (the sons of Bilhah - Dan and Naphtali, and of Zilpah - Gad and Asher) became more intense. Several reasons were likely behind this. Joseph was favored by Jacob. Most likely, he was picked out as the one to receive his father's inheritance (as indicated by the ceremonial robe). He had his father's ear - notice the "bad" reports of 37:2. The "dreams" which Joseph had probably brought the conflict to a head. The "bad report" of 37:2 probably indicates the development in Joseph of a sense of integrity. His father apparently, from time-to-time, sent him on errands to "check-up" on the half-brothers (see 37:12-14). It seems apparent that Joseph "told it like it was" concerning his half-brothers. I choose to see this as an outward manifestation of the development of inner integrity in Joseph - a sense of right and wrong.

Process Item 3. Sense of Destiny

The two dreams given Joseph (37:5-8, 9-11) were the first direct indications of Joseph's own sense of destiny. That there were two dreams with the same focus gave double confirmation and a certainty of God's sovereign intent. It was a prophetic word. From Psalm 105:16-25 and a comparison with the Genesis account, we know that this prophetic word was a word check and a long-term process item of 17 years or so. This word check process item was to form the foundational basis of Joseph's thinking for his life-work and contribution to God's redemptive history. What it all meant was not yet clear to Joseph. Jacob's reaction to this item is interesting and will form the basis for a principle of truth (note especially the last phrase of verse 11).

Process Item 4. Crisis - Sold Into Slavery

Two items mark Joseph's second major personal crisis (Rachel's death was the first one): The "close call with death" and the resultant act of being sold into slavery. This second personal crisis is the boundary item which closes off Phase 1 - Sense of Destiny, Survival. The agony of this experience can be implied from a "chance comment" by the brothers on their first trip to get grain in Egypt. They are talking among themselves. They don't know that Joseph can understand their language. In Genesis 42:21,22, it is recorded:

> They agreed to this and said to one another, "Yes, but now we are suffering the consequences of what we did to our brother (meaning the act of selling Joseph into slavery some 13 or so years earlier - parenthesis mine); we saw the great trouble he was in when he begged for help, but we would not listen. That is why we are in this trouble now." Reuben said, "I told you not to harm the boy, but you wouldn't listen. And now we are being paid back for his death." Joseph understood what they said, but they did not know it, because they had been speaking to him through an interpreter. Joseph left them and began to cry. When he was able to speak again, he came back, picked out Simeon, and had him tied up in front of them. (*Good News Bible*, Gen 42:21-24)

Joseph was isolated geographically and culturally from his foundational upbringing by this boundary process item. But the early lessons of survival of Phase 1 would bring forth fruit in the years that would follow. Joseph had a growing sense of a personal destiny. He could sense God's working in his life.

B. Simple Principle Chart for Phase 1

Name Of Principle	Observation/Event	Principle
Faith Bridge	Sovereign Protection Pattern / The Laban crisis brought on by God's revelation (31:14) and solved by God's revelation (31:14). Joseph clearly saw the hand of God in this confrontation.	1. An early on crisis experience in which God is clearly seen can form the faith bridge for seeing God in later crises where God is not so clearly seen.
Non-deterministic Pattern Phil. 2:15 Light in Darkness	Acts of jelousy and deceit, etc. characterized Joseph's early family upbringing. Joseph stands out even more when against a family background lacking in integrity.	2. a. A person does not have to be bound by an early negative family experience. b. A positive character trait, like integrity stands out, especially when viewed against an environment which conditions negatively against that positive trait.
Sense of Destiny	Peniel experience. Joseph certainly saw the impact of this on Jacob.	3. A family heritage with some sense of destiny experiences can condition one to expect such an experience for oneself.
Context/Birth	Joseph was given in answer to Rachel's prayer	4. A child given in answer to a mother's prayer can expect to be guided by a strong sense of destiny.
Parental Recognition	See Gen 37:9,10,11 where Jacob's reaction to Joseph's dream is given. Notice both the rebuke (vs10) and the pondering (vs11).	5. Parents need to recognize God' personal working with their children so as to encourage and free the children to follow God's Leading.

VI. Joseph's Life: Phase II.

Blessed Buffeting - The Way Up is Down

	A. Integrity & Stewardship		B. Faithful in Little - Faithful in Much		
Location	Egypt - Potiphar's household		Egypt - Jail		
Age	17				30
Boundary		Integrity Crisis			Pharaoh's Dream
Data	Gen 37:36-31:55 Gen 39:1-6	Gen 39:7-23	Gen 39:21-23 Gen 40:1-23 Psa 105:16-25		Gen 41:1-36 Gen 41:37-46
Major Process Items	• Divine Affirmation	• Integrity Check	• Divine Affirmation • Isolation • Word Check	• Divine Contact	•Divine Affirmation •Sovereign Guidance (double confirmation)
Significant Person/ Event	• Potiphar	• Potiphar's Wife Temptation Incident - to Jail	•Jailer	• Wine Steward • Chief Baker Interpretation of dreams - 2 servants	• Pharaoh Interpretation of Pharoah's 2 dreams
Role/ Sphere of Influence	Personal Servant Potiphar	Household Steward Entire Household	Steward Potiphar's holdings all of Potiphar's people	Jail Administrator Prisoners	

A. Narrative Explanation of Detailed Phase II.

Blessing Buffeted

Overview

This development phase represents Joseph's life from 17 to 30. It could be summarized by I Peter 5:6, "Humble yourselves, therefore, under God's mighty hand, that he may lift you in due time." Joseph submitted himself to God in his role in Potiphar's household and in jail. During this period of his life, Joseph was being tested in isolation concerning his personal walk with God. He sensed the presence of God in his life (divine affirmation), learned basic leadership lessons concerning stewardship, passed a crucial test of leadership (classic integrity check), experienced the guidance of God and was exalted by God into a position of extreme importance.

Sub-Phase A. Integrity and Stewardship

Major process items for this sub-phase include:

1. Divine Affirmation
2. Integrity Check

Process Item 1. Divine Affirmation

Usually divine affirmation comes through some external act or a supernatural manifestation of God's presence and approval (e.g. Matt 3:16,17). Joseph's divine affirmation was different. It was an everyday process in which God's favor and approval were seen in the little tasks of life. Outsiders observed the sense of God's presence and blessing on Joseph's everyday life. In the little things that were assigned to him, Joseph was faithful and upright and proved he could be trusted. He was first a personal servant for Potiphar. He did well. Potiphar gave him larger responsibility - management of his household. Again, he proved trustworthy. Potiphar promoted Joseph to head of all his affairs. Gen 39:2,3 makes it clear that the blessing of God was reflected in Joseph's life and seen by Potiphar. Again, the pattern of divine affirmation was seen in the jailer's promotion of Joseph to administrator in the jail. Joseph submitted himself to the situation at hand, did his best at whatever task was given him, and was prospered by God. This sense of God's presence with Joseph, divine affirmation, is highlighted in the Bible commentaries on Joseph's life (see Psa 105:16-25 and Acts 7:9). This process item of divine affirmation in Joseph's life could be summarized in a "bent of life" testimonial, "**God Was With Him!**"

Process Item 2. Integrity Check

The temptation incident with Potiphar's wife is a classic integrity check. Integrity checks are major leadership tests. It should be noticed that Joseph recognized that the sin was more than just a sin against Potiphar, it was against God. Integrity checks in the ultimate are always between God and the individual.

As is often the case with integrity checks, they not only reveal and strengthen inner character but they are also used by God to move a leader forward to a larger sphere of influence. In short, integrity checks are bridges to God's further plans for a life. It was so with Joseph. However, Joseph's expansion required a series of sovereign episodes. And the expansion did not look like expansion for "the way up was first down."

Sub-Phase B. Faithful In Little - Faithful In Much

Major process items for this sub-phase include:

1. Isolation
2. Divine Affirmation
3. Word Check
4. Divine Contact
5. Double Confirmation

Process Item 1. Isolation

The results of Joseph's successful passing of the "Potiphar's Wife Integrity Check" was prison. This illustrates the process item called isolation. Isolation is a setting aside of a person from normal life activities. Isolation processing often involves a setting aside in which the person isolated does not deserve such treatment. Such was the case with Joseph. The isolation is much harder to take when it seemingly is undeserved. Certainly, for Joseph, it was a time for rethinking and evaluating his life. We get something of Joseph's evaluation and inner life emotions in two passages of Scripture - Gen 40:14,15 and Psa 105:18,19. The value of isolation is seen by recognizing it as a time of God's working deeply in the inner-life. Character values are formed in isolation when one can submit to God's purposes in the isolation (especially when the isolation is undeserved).

Process Item 2. Divine Affirmation

Again divine affirmation apparently came through the little things of daily life rather than some special supernatural manifestation. It was clear to the jailer that Joseph's success had upon it the touch of God.

> **But the Lord was with Joseph and blessed him,** so that the jailer was pleased with him. He put Joseph in charge of all the other prisoners and made him responsible for everything that was done in the prison. The jailer did not have to look after anything for which Joseph was responsible, because **the Lord was with Joseph and made him succeed in everything he did.** (Gen 39:21-23)

Joseph gained favor with the prison warden and was promoted to administer all the prisoners. Though Joseph had been unfairly treated he knew God's hand was still upon his life.

Process Item 3. Word Check

The Psa 105:16-25 passage lets us know that the word check process item was taking place.

> *He sent a man before them, even Joseph*
> *who was sold for a servant,*
> *whose feet they hurt with fetters;*
> *He was laid in iron,*
> *until the time that his word came;*
> *The word of the Lord **tested** him.* (Psa 105:17-19)

We do not know how long Joseph was in prison before the incident of the wine steward and baker. But he was in prison for another two years after the incident. During this time in prison (perhaps 2-5 years) he must have remembered the dreams. His faith in that revelation was tried. The word "tried" is a strong word. It is frequently used to describe the refining process of precious metals. It describes the purifying process whereby the precious metals are separated from dross. Joseph himself (his faith) and the word of God were on trial. Had it been a word from God? Could he, in the lowest point in his life, believe God would do it? How could God make it happen for someone in prison? Most likely, there were many questions that flooded Joseph's mind during the lonely hours of prison isolation. He could have easily blamed God for the injustices (40:15).

Process Item 4.
Divine Contact - the Link into Pharaoh's Court

The incident of the two dreams in chapter 40 is an illustration of the "left-hand of God" at work. God gave dreams to Pharaoh's wine steward and baker. Joseph recognized these dreams as providential (40:8). Joseph gave the interpretations. They came true just as Joseph predicted.[33] Joseph told the wine steward of

---

33 This must have been an encouragement to Joseph that his own dream would come true. Probably, this was part of the "trying" process of Joseph's own word check.

his own situation and asked him to appeal to Pharaoh for justice for himself (40:14). Even though Joseph, himself, was forgotten, this ability to interpret dreams was not (40:23, 41;9-13). The wine steward became a "divine contact," a person used by God to significantly influence Joseph's destiny.

Process Item 5. Double Confirmation
Sovereign Guidance, Pharaoh's Two Dreams

Joseph recognized the two dreams as one and coming from God (the double confirmation principle, 41:25,32). He made sure that Pharaoh knew that God was the one behind the dreams (41:16,25,28,32). Pharaoh's response (41:38-44) was key to God's use of this process item to move Joseph into a key position. From that position, God would use Joseph to deliver Jacob and his descendants from the famine. This would fulfill part of the prophecy given to Abraham (Gen 15:13f). Again, the "left hand of God" is to be working in his use of Pharaoh as a means for deliverance of his people. This "promotion for Joseph" set the stage for the fulfillment of Joseph's own dreams given to him as a lad of 17. It had been 13 years since those dreams were given. It would be another 9 before they were fulfilled entirely. This "guidance process item" which propelled Joseph to a top political position was the boundary event which closed off Development Phase II, Blessing Buffeting - The Way Up Is Down.

B. Principle Chart - Phase II.
Blessed Buffeting

Name of Principle	Observation	Principle
Daily Divine Affirmation	Gen 39:1-3 & 21-23. It is interesting to note that Joseph's daily testimony was recognized by non-believers as having God's presence & blessing.	6. Divine affirmation can be seen in the daily activities of life (an exemplary character, success in tasks) as well as spectacular revelations.
Integrity Essence	Gen 39:9 ... and sin against God	7. Integrity in its essence is an inner reckoning with God concerning rightness of conscience.
Prophetic Word Check	Gen 37:5-7, 9-11; 42:9	8. A word check may be processed over a long time interval.
		9. In its intent a word check may not not be initially clear (although its origin may be sure).
Divine Contacts	Gen 40:22 God's interpretation of the two dreams in jail.	10. Expect God to give encouragement to faith during the process of a long interval word check.
	Gen 40. Wine steward - link between Joseph (in prison) and Pharaoh in his palace.	11. A divine contact does not necessarily have to be a person of God, but one that God uses to significantly influence another at a strategic time.
Double Confirmation Essence	Gen 41:25. The dream of Pharaoh is one: God has shown Pharaoh what he is about to do. 41:32. And for that dream was doubled unto Pharaoh twice; it is because the thing is <u>established by God</u> and God will shortly bring it to pass.	12. God can establish guidance clearly by repeated confirmation of it.
Isolation Kinds	Gen 37:28; 39:20	13. Isolation can be geographical, familial, cultural, or vocational.

VII. Joseph's Life: Phase III.
Destiny Fulfilled - The Faith Act

	A. Pre-Famine	B. Famine	C. Deliverance	D. Celebration
Location	Egypt	Egypt	Egypt	
Age	30			110?
Boundary	Lean years Start	Jacob's Double Confirmation (Beersheba)		
Data	Gen 41:47-57	Gen 42:1-38 Gen 43:1-34 Gen 44:1-45:28	Gen 46:1-33 Gen 47 Acts 7:9-15 Gen 48 Psa 105:16-25 Gen 49:1-50:3 Gen 50:4-12	Gen 50:15-21 Heb 11:22 Gen 50:22-26
Major Process Items	• Word Check (Pharaoh's Dreams	• Word Check (Joseph's Dreams)	• Sense of Destiny • Integrity Check (brothers) • Divine Affirmation	• Integrity Check (brothers) • Faith - Act
Significant Person/ Event	• Reuben	• Benjamin/reunion • Judah	• Jacob/Prophet Blessing • Jacob's death/burial • Convergence	Joseph's burial wish
Role/ Sphere of Influence	• Ruler of all Egypt under Pharaoh		• Ruler of all Egypt under Pharaoh • Deliverer/Israel	

A. Narrative Explanation of Detailed Phase III. Destiny Fulfilled

Overview

This development phase represents Joseph's life from age 30 to 110. It could be summarized by the underlined phrase of I Peter 5:6:

> *Humble yourselves, therefore, under God's mighty hand, that **He may lift you in due time.***

Joseph's time had come. God was going to use Joseph to deliver Abraham's descendants as he had promised years before (Gen 15). God had now placed Joseph in a position where that deliverance could be accomplished. He would also fulfill the prophetic word given to Joseph (Gen 37). Not much is given concerning the majority of time involved in this phase. The major process items that arise during this final development phase include:

1. Word Check (Pharaoh's two dreams - faith check)
2. Word Check (own - fulfilled)
3. Sense of Destiny (Joseph saw the purpose of God in his life)
4. Integrity Check (brothers)
5. Integrity Check (Jacob)
6. Divine Affirmation
7. Final Integrity Check (brothers)
8. Faith Check (demonstrated in faith/act - death wish)

Sub-Phase A. Pre-Famine

Process Item 1. Word Check

Joseph had interpreted Pharaoh's dreams. He had gone out on a limb and claimed that the interpretations were from God. He now acts upon that faith and sets his plan of gathering grain and saving it into action. The seven years of plenty occurred just exactly as Joseph had predicted.

Sub-Phase B. Famine

Process Item 2. Fulfillment of Word Check

Just as predicted, the seven years of famine followed the years of plenty. As the famine worsened, Joseph's plan for storing grain during the years of plenty proved to be wisdom indeed. His further planning insured survival for the people of Egypt, as well as increasing the Pharaoh's land holdings. During this sub-phase, Jacob's sons made their trips to Egypt. Joseph's own word check had begun 22 years previous (Gen 37) came to fulfillment. It was a long process item. Joseph's faith concerning that word given in the two dreams of Gen 37 was tested and found to be pure.

Sub-Phase C. Deliverance

Several process items are noted in this sub-phase. They include the final clarification of the intent of Joseph's word check - the fulfilling of God's deliverance for Jacob. The trek back to the land to bury Jacob foreshadowed Joseph's own final wish and underlined the importance of getting back to the land as a God had promised. Passages outside of Genesis comment on the main thrust of this period of Joseph's life. Both Psalms 105:16-25 and Acts 7:9-15 highlight divine affirmation in Joseph's life. Both point out that, in spite of hardships, it was clear that "God was with Joseph" and was directing toward a destiny.

Process Item 3. Sense of Destiny

It became clear to Joseph how God had been working through the ups and downs of his life to deliver Jacob's descendants as well as save many others from the famine. In retrospect, Joseph was able to see the hand of God superintending the various events which led up to the deliverance of Jacob and his family.

Process Items 4 and 7. Integrity Check - Brothers

During the famine sub-phase, the deliverance sub-phase and the celebration sub-phase, Joseph underwent integrity checks concerning his brothers. It was clear that they expected him to take vengeance for their early hostile acts to Joseph. But Joseph's inner character showed him to be a person who submitted to God's purposes in those early acts. He did not use his authority and power to exact revenge but instead modeled a lifestyle that would later be taught in the New Testament. Joseph's answers to his brothers during these checks are worth noting.

Joseph said to his brothers, "I am Joseph. Is my father still alive?" But when his brothers heard this, they were so terrified that they could not answer. Then Joseph said to them, "Please come closer." They did, and he said, "I am your brother Joseph, whom you sold into Egypt. Now do not be upset or blame yourselves because you sold me here. It was really God who sent me here ahead of you to save people's lives. This is only the second year of famine in the land; there will be five more years in which there will be neither plowing nor reaping. God sent me ahead of you to rescue you in this amazing way and to make sure that you and your descendants will survive. So it was not really you that sent me here, but God. He has made me the king's highest official. I am in charge of his whole country; I am the ruler of all Egypt." *(Good News Bible,* Genesis 45:3-8*)*

After the death of Jacob, the final aspect of this integrity check took place. The character of the brothers and Joseph's own character stand in sharp contrast.

After the death of their father, Joseph's brothers said, "What if Joseph still hates us and plans to pay us back for all the harm we did him?" So they sent a message to Joseph: "Before our father died, he told us to ask you, 'Please forgive the crime your brothers committed when they wronged you.' Now please forgive us the wrong that we, the servants of your father's God, have done." Joseph cried when he received this message. (*Good News Bible*, Genesis 50:15-17)

The brothers had lived all the years of the deliverance sub-phase near Joseph and yet they still did not know his inner character. They assumed he was like them. If the positions had been reversed, they would have taken vengeance. Note that they are deceitful (at least that is my assumption) in their appeal to Joseph. They use their father (Jacob probably never said what they claimed) as leverage to hope to persuade Joseph. But Joseph was different. He operated on a different set of inner principles. Note his response. He cried. They did not understand the workings of God whom they claimed to serve nor his servant Joseph.

But Joseph said to them, "Don't be afraid; I can't put myself in the place of God. You plotted evil against me, but God turned it into good, in order to preserve the lives of many people who are alive today because of what happened. You have nothing to fear. I will take care of you and your children. So he reassured them with kind words that touched their hearts. (*Good News Bible*, Genesis 50:19-21)

Process Item 5. Integrity Check - Jacob's Death Wish

Jacob made Joseph take a solemn oath to bury him back in the land of Canaan. Joseph fulfilled the oath. In doing so, he was modeling what he wanted done in his own case some years later. He was also keeping alive the importance of the promised land and the ultimate return there.

Process Item 6. Divine Affirmation

Joseph's success as minister of economics hinged directly on his understanding of God's revelations via the dreams. It was clear, as the famine developed, that God gave Joseph wisdom to meet the situation. Two major comments on this period of Joseph's life highlights the divine presence and purpose (see Psalms 105:16-25 and Acts 7:9-15). The essence of the divine affirmation process item is the assurance of the presence of God and of his blessing on a life. That is exactly what is emphasized in both commentaries.

Process Item 8. Faith-Check

Joseph, in his death-wish to be buried back in the promised land when the Lord took the children of Israel back, demonstrated his belief in God's prophetic word. This was a faith act which was to keep before the children of Israel God's intent to carry them back to the promised land. It was a final faith/act which was to influence the children of Israel for over 400 years. It is this faith/act which is cited in Hebrews 11:22. Joshua 24:32 shows the end result of the faith/act, and the impact of Joseph's influence.

B. Principle Chart - Phase III. Destiny Fulfilled

Name of Principle	Observation	Principle
Faith-Act	Joseph made plans based on his relevatory gifts. In retrospect it looks simple enough. But in prospect it is often frightening. What if Joseph was wrong on Pharaoh's dreams.	14. Faith manifests itself in firm plans and actions which risk failure.
Affirmation Guidelines	Joseph's divine affirmation items in all three phases. Comparison of Abraham's, Joseph's, Samuel's and Jesus' divine affirmation process items.	15.a. Christian workers need divine affirmation. It is not wrong to want it. b. Be sensitive to the ways it might come. Expect affirmation in the little things of life as well as unusual God events. c. Reflect back on divine affirmation experiences to see God's patterns for you and to renew your faith. d. Expect God to transition (wean) you from sight to faith.
Affirmation Symptoms	Comparison of divine process items of Abraham, Joseph, Samuel, Jesus	16. Symptoms indicating need for divine affirmation and leading toward expectancy of same: a. A promise that has been long in coming. (Abraham) b. In an isolation situation where no other believers are and where encouragement is needed. (Joseph) c. There is a need for external proof in order to give authority to ministry. (Samuel) d. The need for inner assurance that what you are doing is contributing to God's kingdom. (Jesus) e. There is a time of indecision (boundary condition) and a need to be reassurred by God while the process of guidance is going on.
Word Check Guidelines	Observation of Joseph's word check	17.a. Word checks are God's means for mixing faith with understanding and result in a person more sensitive to God's dynamic revelation. b. Word checks may process for a long period of time. c. Expect God to test, clarify, and expand your ability to hear Him to give you a personal word. d. Word checks may not initially be clear as to understanding of details and may be clarified over time. However, the source of the word check can be certain to the eye of faith. e. A word check on which there is closure not only expands your experential knowledge of God but sources as a stimulant to spiritual authority. f. Joseph's personal word check involved several stages: (1) *The Tender Touch*: when there is the excitment of knowing the living God has given the word characterized by naive enthusiasm. (2) *The Testing of Time*: The tough period is characterized by not seeing any of the word in reality around you. This may last for a long period. (3) *The Touchstone Time*: a crisis time when by faith you assert that the word is true whether or not you see it. You go back and reaffirm the original word by faith. (4) *The Triumphant Testimoney Time*: Celebration as the word check unfolds and God's purposes are fufilled

B. Principle Chart - Phase III. Destiny Fulfilled cont.

Name of Principle	Observation	Principle
Integrity Check	Joseph's integrity items in all three development phases.	18. a. Integrity is a key essential of leadership. b. Integrity in essence is an inner thing between God and the leader. The surface situation only points to the real issue. c. Expect integrity to be checked throughout your lifetime. d. Integrity checks not only build inner character but also are used as further stepping stones to expanded usefulness by God. e. The immediate results of the successful passing of an integrity check may appear to be demotion not expansion of sphere of influence.
Convergence	Reflection on the various factors that converged in Joseph's third development phase.	19. a. Every phase in one's process contains some convergence and leads toward greater convergence to one sensitive to God in everyday life. b. When there is a possible choice make a decision based on your understanding of convergence. c. Factors which converged for Joseph: (1) sovereign guidance (2) prophetic word fulfilled (3) stewardship experience/integrity (4) role/minister of economics (5) sphere of influence (6) sense of destiny fulfilled (7) geographical location (8) giftedness/revelatory gifts, wisdom
Leadership observations	Comparison of Joseph's time-line with basic leadership ideas seen elsewhere in Scripture.	20 a. Joseph highlights integrity as an essential of leadership which God affirms. b. Capacity to influence, responsibility, directedness, focus of influence, all are reflected in Joseph's leadership selection process. c. A leader must influence in such a way as to encourage faith in an unseen God. He must demonstrate the presence and power of God. d. Power can be manifest via revelatory gifts as well as healing, power praying, and other miraculous authentications. e. A leader must encourage followers so that there is expectancy and hope for the future. Joseph's long-term leadership influence (the faith-act) did just that.

VIII. CONCLUSIONS

In the beginning of my study I laid out six expectations:

1. To see the "left-hand of God" at work and to note the process items which correlate with the providential working (Gen 45:5,7; 50:2; Psa 105:17; Acts 7:9,10)

2. To study the concept "sense of destiny" and identify essential elements of that concept as reflected in Joseph's life.

3. To reflect on the generalized time-line phases to see how Joseph's unique time-line reflects these generalized phases.

4. To expand my understanding of several major process items, among which are: word check, sovereign guidance (double confirmation), sense of destiny, etc.

5. To identify in seed form some essentials of leadership.

6. To list some observations concerning leadership principles.

How have I done? Did I meet those expectations? In this concluding section, I will comment on each of the six expectations. In addition, I will discuss other observations beyond those expectations.

Expectation 1

The "left hand of God" can probably be more concisely defined in light of observations of its effect in Joseph's life. The "left hand of God" is God's indirect use of people and events to accomplish His purposes. The people will usually have little or no idea that what they are doing is related to God or his purposes. The events, in themselves, may have every appearance of not relating to God. But in retrospect, a study of the events and actions of the people and final results reveals that the purposes of God were accomplished. And He brought his purpose to pass not violating the "free-will" of the unknowing participants.

Genesis 12 and 15 alert us to some of God's long range purposes. God is purposing to use Abraham and his descendants to bless the world. The prophetic passage of Genesis 15 indicates that those descendants will be in Egypt and will be delivered by God. They will be in Egypt for over 400 years and then brought back to the promised land. Joseph plays an important role in part of these plans. He will be used to preserve Jacob's descendants. What were some of the indications of "God's left hand at work?" And what were the process items in Joseph's life which related to that working? Can these same kinds of process items be used today in the lives of emerging leaders in the same kinds of ways. Table 1 gives a list reflecting findings concerning the "left hand of God" in Joseph's life.

Table 1. Left-hand of God Incidents & Process Items

Event/Person	Process Item	Purpose	Explanation
Joseph's Birth	sense of destiny - special name reminding of God	unique person to be used by God	Joseph is born in answer to prayer and in God's timing. Rachel is seeking to satisfy her own needs. God teaches her concerning her poor attitude toward Leah. The late date of Joseph's arrival plus being the firstborn of Rachel. The late date of Joseph's arrival plus being the firstborn of Rachel assures Joseph of first place with Jacob an issue which will culminate in Joseph's eventual departure to Egypt.
Reuben, Judah	Crisis - Joseph's trip to brothers their violent attitude towards him	preserve Joseph's life	Rueben's intent in suggesting that the brother's throw Joseph in the well was to preserve his life and send him back to Jacob. In his absence Judah further persuaded the brothers not to kill Joseph but sell him to the Ishmaelites. That way they would gain money and be rid of Joseph in the family - yet preserve his life.
Ishmaelite traders on way to Egypt	Sovereign Guidance	get Joseph to Egypt	Coincidently (providentially) the traders appear and prompt Judah's suggestion which will preserve Joseph's life as well as get him to Egypt - the place where God will greatly use Joseph.
sold to Potiphar	divine affirmation	train Joseph in stewardship and administration, integrity; put in upper class environment	Joseph could have been put into any household but it was an upperclass household with connections into royal leadership. It was Potiphar who also recognized the "blessing of God" upon Joseph's life in whatever task he set himself to do whether personal servant, household manager, or estate manager.
incident with Potiphar's wife	interity check/ soverign guidence	point out essential leadership trait of intergrity	The classical integrity check becomes a watershed in deepening Joseph's inner character as well as a bridge to sovereignly guide Joseph to the place where God will provide the divine contact into the Egyptian palace.
Jail situation	divine affirmation	train further in stewardship, administration; located in prison for royal prisoners	The jailer was a person who could recognize leadership and was willing to delegate. He too, like Potiphar, recognized Joseph's day to day administrative success as being "the blessing of God."
baker and wine steward	divine contact	stepping stone to palace	God uses the baker and wine steward who have been put into prison by Pharaoh. God gives them their dreams and gives Joseph the interpretation to those dreams. This incident, especially the fact that the dreams came true just as Joseph predicted, will later give Joseph credibility as a person with revelatory giftedness. His ability to manage wisely the administration of the jail will also serve him well.
Pharaoh's dreams	sovereign guidance	to promote Joseph, to deliver people from the famine, to bring Jacob's family to Egypt and fulfill Joseph's prophetic word as well as fulfill the Abrahamic prophecy	God gave Pharaoh the two dreams (double confirmation) meaning the same thing. Pharaoh was impressed that the dreams were supernatural. The wine steward "remembered" his jail dream and Joseph. Joseph was catapulted into the top position of authority under Pharaoh when he interpreted the dreams and gave wisdom as to how to face the situation.

Both natural events and supernatural events are used to reflect "the left hand of God."

Natural Events, Institutions, Relationships

- mother's desire for a child
- jealousy of brothers
- trader's caravan
- institution of slavery
- a woman's desire
- curiosity about dreams
- jail

Supernatural Events

- timing of birth
- dreams
- interpretation of dreams
- prophetic foretelling

Of particular interest are the dreams. It is clear that God was behind both the giving of dreams and the giving of interpretations. He was sovereignly controlling and pointing out what He would do.

People of all kinds are used. Relatives, traders, upper class, lower class and royalty itself all serve God's purposes in promoting Joseph from a tribal son to a ruler.

Those personally related to Joseph, such as his mother and brothers, operate with their own desires and for their own ends, yet, are used by God for God's purposes. The Ishmaelite traders on their way from Gilead to Egypt buy Joseph at a bargain price and later sell him making their profit but also providing God's free transportation for Joseph to Egypt.

God is going to use Joseph as ruler of all Egypt. He will need to be enculturated into Egyptian upper class thinking and ways. Potiphar, an upper class man of rank, prestige and connections, serves this purpose. He is used to recognize Joseph's leadership qualities and to enculturate Joseph into the upper class thought patterns and ways of acting. He learns basic Egyptian economy while managing Potiphar's household. Potiphar's wife, following her own natural desires and for her own purposes, tempts Joseph. Her reactions to his rejection sets the stage for Joseph's imprisonment. Not just to any prison, but to the royal prison - where Joseph will contact the wine steward.

The jailer recognizes Joseph's leadership. He is a man who can delegate and thus allows Joseph to administrate the jail affairs. The wine steward, not just any wine steward but Pharaoh's, is used as a divine contact to bring Joseph to the attention of Pharaoh.

Pharaoh, himself, is given two dreams by God. These dreams impress Pharaoh as supernatural and having divine significance. The wine steward provides the key which will unlock Pharaoh's dreams. He remembers Joseph and thus provides the link which will enable Joseph to move into power.

It is clear that people of all kinds pursuing their ends can be used of God for His own purposes. Family members, differing racial groups, employers, fellow-sufferers and royalty all played their part in Joseph's destiny.

Two final observations stand out to me concerning the "left-hand" of God. One, Joseph submitted himself in the terrible circumstances. He never became bitter toward God because of them. He simply used his God-given abilities to do the best job he could in the circumstances. Two, each situation was an opportunity to see God work. Joseph knew the presence of God in the little things of life.

Expectation 2. Sense of Destiny Observations

It is clear in retrospect that Joseph saw himself as a person of destiny.

> Now do not be upset or blame yourselves because you sold me here. It was really God who sent me ahead of you to save people's lives. (*Good News Bible*, Gen 45:5)

> You plotted evil against me, but God turned it into good. (*Good News Bible*, Gen 50:20)

It is not as clear just how much he realized his sense of destiny as the events were unfolding. What can be learned about the sense of destiny process item by reflecting on Joseph's leadership selection process? Look at my earlier definition.

A sense of destiny experience is defined as a unique awe-inspiring experience:

- in which God reveals Himself,
- to an obedient surrendered follower,
- in order to inspire/ lead that person on to accomplish something special in his/her lifetime.

As far as the Biblical record goes, we see that Joseph had only one experience which matches the above definition. That would be the "ruler dreams" of Genesis 37. Yet, it is also clear from Joseph's own testimony given above and the Bible commentaries on Joseph's life, Psa 105 and Acts 7, that Joseph was a person of destiny. This lack of spectacular sense of destiny experiences coupled with the fact that the Bible clearly marks Joseph as a person of destiny suggests that special insights can be gained from careful reflection using a sense of destiny focus. Two areas of clarification are suggested to me. One concerns the process of recognizing and entering into a sense of destiny. The second concerns a broadening of the present definition of sense of destiny.

What factors were involved in developing that sense of destiny? I note eight observations that contributed either directly or indirectly to Joseph's understanding of a sense of destiny and his own entering into such a life.

1) He sensed he was part of a Godly heritage (following the God of Abraham, Isaac and Jacob and not the gods of Laban, for example).

2) He was familiar with ways in which sense of destiny experiences occurred in the lives of Abraham, Isaac and Jacob. He would have heard the stories about Abraham's call, Isaac's birth and near sacrifice and Jacob's ladder, etc. He was thus conditioned by a sense of Godly heritage and knowing how God had intervened with his great-grandfather, grandfather and father. He would be sensitive to such a destiny himself. (But why were not his brothers just as sensitive?)

3) He was there when his father had major sense of destiny experiences (Peniel and Bethel).

4) He saw evidence of sovereign protection of his family. (Laban crisis).

5) He knew he, himself, was an answer to prayer. (Gen 30:24).

6) He had a personal experience with God (prophetic word given in dreams).

7) He knew his own life had been preserved (the slavery crisis).

8) His daily life, working at whatever tasks he was given, reflected the presence and blessing of God so as to be recognized by others. (Gen 39:2,3; 2123)

Some of these kinds of factors will reappear in other leadership studies. We should at least be aware of a variety of ways in which

God intervenes in the destiny of a leader. They might well apply in our own lives. They may give us insights as we help develop other leaders.

There is a second thing we learn about sense of destiny. In addition to learning how one becomes sensitized to the concept of sense of destiny, we expand our understanding of the definition itself. As far as we know, Joseph had one direct major sense of destiny experience - the ruler dreams of Gen 37. This was probably the root experience upon which other minor elements were founded to build an increased sense of destiny. An accumulation of sovereign guidance experiences (seen most likely when reflecting back) and a personal sense of God being with him in all that he did contributed to growing sense of destiny. It is probably this "divine assurance" which most contributed to Joseph's growing sense of destiny. The Bible makes it clear that it was God who blessed Joseph and made him prosper in all that he did. The indirect data passages in Psa 105 and Acts 7 also focus on this theme of divine assurance - God was with him. So then we can summarize that Joseph's life indicates that a sense of destiny process item is more than just an awe-inspiring experience. It is not bound to one point in time but can be expanded into a series of experiences. It can be a process as well as an act. So then we can refine the definition.

Definition: A *sense of destiny* process item is a unique awe-inspiring act or series of experiences through which it becomes clear:

- that God has revealed Himself,
- to an obedient follower,
- in order to inspire (lead or sovereignly direct) that person on to accomplish something special in his/her lifetime.

Thus it becomes clear through Joseph's life that an accumulation of sovereign guidance experiences and divine affirmation experiences indicate sense of destiny as well as the spectacular awe-inspiring acts.

Expectation 3. Generalized Time Line

The generalized time line lists 6 major development thrusts:

1. Sovereign Foundations
2. Inner-life Growth
3. Ministry Maturing
4. Life Maturing
5. Convergence
6. Afterglow (Celebration)

Joseph's leadership data study does not provide enough evidence to see all as these thrusts nor to link each of them directly to some one development phase in Joseph's life. However, some observations can be noted.

The sovereign foundations stage is very crucial to the Joseph leadership selection process. Many process items listed under sovereign foundations are seen in Joseph's life. These are listed under his Development Phase I, Seeds of Destiny and were discussed at length in the narratives describing Phase I.

Inner-life Growth process items occur primarily in Joseph's Phase II, Blessed Buffeting. The classic integrity check and the word check are examples of inner-life growth items.

Ministry maturing is seen in both Phases II and III. Joseph develops in integrity concerning management of another's affairs (stewardship). He is seen as a person who can be trusted to handle someone else's affairs. He is obviously successful in administration as he is given larger responsibilities as time goes by. His success is attributed directly to God's presence and blessing of his life. This element is key in any ministry maturing— that is, the recognition of God's accomplishment through one.

We see little of Life-Maturing except for the jail experience. That isolation process item must have deepened Joseph's own convictions concerning God and the trustworthiness of His word.

Phase III, Destiny Fulfilled, probably yields the most helpful information toward understanding the Generalized Time line. It helps us understand the generalized time line thrust of Convergence. It is clear that Development Phase III contains convergence for Joseph. The Bible commentary indicates that Joseph fulfilled a sense of destiny toward which he had been directed all his life. Factors that are highlighted in Joseph's convergence include:

1. Prophetic word—a prophecy can undergird one's inner-life during the process toward convergence and can be used as a touchstone during major career decisions and boundary transitions.

2. Experience—Joseph's final role utilized his previous "stewardship" training and experience. His track record concerning integrity showed that he could be trusted to control other peoples' wealth and power for their good.

3. Role—Joseph was elevated to the highest role (2nd only to Pharaoh) and in a practical sense the first since day-to-day running of the country was left to him. The role fit his experience and giftedness. His understanding of God's purposes (revelatory gift, and wisdom gift) contributed greatly to his administrative plans.

4. Sphere of influence—Joseph's sphere of influence increased until it matched his God-given abilities.

5. Divine affirmation and sovereign guidance— Joseph was directed sovereignly over events over which he had little control until he was in the place and position of God's choosing. And in each place God gave assurance of His presence and blessing to Joseph.

6. Geography—the right location is usually crucial to convergence since certain roles and spheres of influence will depend upon centers of communication, control, and power. Such was the case with Joseph.

7. Importance of sense of destiny—Convergence for Joseph was in terms of fulfilling purpose in God's larger plan toward which Joseph had been directed all his life.

8. Giftedness—One can not talk about "spiritual gifts" in the same sense that can be spoken of in New Testament church life since Joseph was primarily exercising leadership in a secular context. But it is clear that Joseph was free to exercise his administrative ability, to use his wisdom, to depend upon his understanding of God's supernatural revelation. Not only was he free to do so in his role as minister of economic affairs but his role enhanced the use of these gifts.

Those not normally stressed in convergence and which should be noted as expanding an understanding of convergence are the place of the prophetic word, the need for divine affirmation, being in the right location, and the sense of fulfilling a sense of destiny.

Expectation 4—Expanding Understanding on Process Items

I was helped in my understanding of the following process items:

1. Sense of destiny,
2. Word check.
3. Sovereign guidance (especially double confirmation),
4. Divine affirmation.

I have already discussed sense of destiny (Expectation 1 on pages 48-52) so I will not say anything further on it.

In terms of understanding word check I have listed my expanded understandings in the Principle Chart Phase III, page 46, under the principle of word check guidelines. The primary insights I gained concerning word checks were two: (1) recognizing that word checks my be over a lengthy time (2) seeing the process unfold—I listed 4 stages to the process; see Principle 17.f. on page 46.

The classic divine affirmation usually comes through some external act or a supernatural manifestation of God's presence and approval such as the voice on the Mount of Transfiguration. Joseph helped me to see the essence of the divine affirmation process item—the sensed presence of God. In Joseph's case, he knew he was in the right place. For his location and functions were controlled by sovereign guidance. He submitted himself in those situations and saw God's blessing in the little tasks of life. The divine presence was sensed by those around him. Joseph was given (at least as far as is recorded in the Bible record) very little in the way of supernatural divine affirmation. It was primarily natural—that is, sensed in the daily routine of life.

Sovereign guidance for Joseph came primarily through the "left-hand of God." See especially Table 1 on page 50. However, in two cases it is clear that sovereign guidance was in the form of the special process item called double confirmation. The classic double confirmation item is seen in the Paul and Ananias incident in Acts 9. There guidance is given to one party and confirmed through a second party. Here, in Joseph's case the double confirmation is given twice to the same person. The essence of the definition is highlighted, that is, two different items meaning the same thing and repeated to focus on the idea of confirmation from God. The repeated emphasis insures that the guidance is certain and from God. In Gen. 37, Joseph gets two different dreams from God on two different occasions. They both contain the same meaning. The reinforcement indicates the certainty with which it will happen. Joseph is deeply impressed that the dreams are from God and are part of his destiny. But he is not certain of the details. He knew he would rule but not when or how or how wide his rule would be. It is in interpreting Pharaoh's two dreams that the essence of double confirmation is highlighted.

> *Joseph said to the king, "The two dreams mean the same thing" God has told you what he is going to do."* (Gen 41:25)

> *The repetition of your dream means that the*
> *matter is fixed by God and that he will make it*
> *happen in the near future.*   (Gen 41:25)

The bottom-line of my expanded understanding of the double confirmation process item is the following. In Major Decisions A Leader Can Trust God To Give Repeated Confirmation.

Expectations 5 and 6.
Essentials of Leadership/Observations

I use the following leadership definition to guide me in my analysis of leaders.

A leader is a person,

1. Who has a God-given capacity to influence,
2. Who senses a God-given responsibility to influence,
3. Who influences a specific group of God's people,
4. Who influences them toward God's purposes for the group.

Joseph manifests something of each of the 4 characteristics of leadership. I have summed up my leadership observations on page 47 under principle 20. Let me reiterate 3 items.

Joseph highlights integrity as an essential leadership trait. Integrity is at the heart of a leader's credibility to lead. It is a capacity that is developed in the interplay between God's truth and life which tests that truth. Integrity tests are primarily for the benefit of the one tested. They reveal to that one inner character and fiber that can be depended upon on future situations. Usually they are bridges signaling capacity for larger things.

Joseph influenced in such a way as to encourage faith in an unseen God. He demonstrated the power and presence of God. Who can reveal the future? Who can control it? Who is directing the course of history? Only God can. But God is not seen. A leader functions to point to this unseen God and inspire confidence in Him. This Joseph did. He interpreted God's revelation through dreams. He carried out large plans based on these interpretations. And the interpretations were true. His plans worked. God was honored and His purposed fulfilled.

Not only must a leader be a person of integrity and inspire followers to know the unseen God but he/she must encourage followers so that there is expectancy and hope for the future. Life is comprised of much that is routine, unexciting, even tragic. A leader can see through and beyond this to the broader purposes of God. He must encourage others in the midst of a non-encouraging world to believe that God is moving toward His purposes. Joseph's final leadership act epitomizes this leadership essential. It was a faith-act, that is, an act which publicly demonstrated confidence that God would do something. Joseph's wish that he be carried back and buried in the land gave faith to God's promise that He would someday carry the descendants of Jacob back into the land. The Joshua 24:32 passage and the Hebrews 11:22 passage emphasize the influence of this leadership act by Joseph. The leadership influence of this final faith-act lasted for nearly 400 years.

In summary then, some of the essentials of leadership seen in Joseph include:

1. Capacity to influence (both inherent and developed),

2. Responsibility to influence (he accepted each new leadership task and did it to the best of his ability),

3. Recognized the groups and elements for which he was accountable and to whom accountable (Potiphar, Jailer, Pharaoh, ultimately God),

4. Moved toward God's purposes on each leadership task (doing the small tasks as unto the Lord, the larger tasks in light of revelation),

5. Encouraged those influenced to believe in the power and presence of the living and unseen God (personally modeled this and made leadership decisions based on his understanding of this God),

6. Instilled hope and expectancy for the future and hence gave meaning to endurance of the present.

I close my study by giving my interpretation of Joseph's ultimate testimony—that is the bent of his life. I do it symbolically—using the tombstone which follows. His ultimate testimony, at least in part, should be reflected in all leaders!

JOSEPH

**SON OF JACOB
GRANDSON OF ISAAC
GREAT-GRANDSON OF ABRAHAM**

Born: Mesopotamia
Died: Egypt
Buried: Shechem
Age: 110

...BUT GOD WAS WITH HIM

He saw God's hand and ultimate
purposes in the reversals of life
and God exalted him.

I PETER 5: 6

Appendix A. List of Vignettes
JOSEPH
Direct Data

Vignettes	Scripture	Topic/Process Items/Comments
1	Gen 37:2	Incident with Brothers/INTEGRITYJoseph willing to go against the grain where principles and integrity are at stake
2	Gen 37:3,4	Favoritism/FAMILY; CONFLICT/see Handout Sheet detailing family relationships
3	Gen 37:5-8	Sheaf Dream/SENSE OF DESTINY, WORD CHECK, Joseph sensed that these dreams were from God
4	Gen 37:9-11	Sun, Moon, Stars Dream/SENSE OF DESTINY, DOUBLE CONFIRMATION/two such dreams indicate double confirmation
5	Gen 37:12-35	Sold Into Slavery/SOVEREIGN GUIDANCE (Egypt)/divine contact Reuben saves Joseph's life
6	Gen 37:36 Gen 39:1-6	Steward for Potiphar/SOVEREIGN GUIDANCE, DIVINE AFFIRMATION/It is clear that God's hand is upon Joseph and he is promoted to head steward of Potiphar's household within a few short years.
7	Gen 39:7-23	Potiphar's wife--Temptation/IINTEGRITY CHECK/ Joseph passes the integrity check; he sees it in relation to God no matter what others thought or knew.
8	Gen 39:21-23	Jail/ISOLATION, DIVINE AFFIRMATION/God is beginning the promotion from the previous integrity check. He has Joseph in the place from which He will bring top-level divine contacts.
9	Gen 40:1-23	JAIL/REVELATION - WORD TESTING DIVINE CONTACTS/ See Psa 105:28; Joseph will get a reputation for interpreting dreams which God will use to place him in the highest role in the land under Pharaoh.
10	Gen 41:1-36	Pharaoh's Dreams/SOVEREIGN GUIDANCE, ROLE MATCH/God now uses Joseph to interpret the dreams and promotes him to the highest role in land.
11	Gen 41:37-46	Role Match/SOVEREIGN GUIDANCE, DIVINE AFFIRMATION, SPHERE OF INFLUENCE/The first part of Joseph's initial word check (2 dreams) is now fulfilled. Joseph is in a ruler position.
12	Gen 41:47-57	Preparation for famine/WORD CHECK/Joseph relies on God's word though circumstances around him belie any famine to come.
13	Gen 42:1-38	Brother's first trip/WORD CHECK - Celebration/2nd half of Joseph's original 2 dreams is fulfilled; it is becoming clear to Joseph now of God's intent in the whole process.
14	Gen 43:1-34	Brother's 2nd visit/WORD CHECK - Celebration/Joseph works toward God's purposes in the process.
15	Gen 44:1-45:28	Benjamin and silver cup/WORD CHECK/Joseph tests brothers and sees Judah's integrity

Appendix A. List of Vignettes Cont.
JOSEPH
Direct Data

Vignettes	Scripture	Topic/Process Items/Comments
16	Gen 46:1-33	Jacob's vision at Beersheeba/DOUBLE CONFIRMATION/God is providentially saving His people and gives a major guidance check to Jacob.
17	Gen 47:1-12	Jacob meets Pharoah/SENSE OF DESTINY/ God's final solution is now clear. Pharaoh gives Jacob's family good land and his protection. Jacob blesses Pharoah.
18	Gen 47:13-26	Famine increases/ CONVERGENCE/Joseph wisely manages through the crisis.
19	Gen 47:27-31	Jacob demands vow from Joseph/INTEGRITY CHECK/Jacob demands a sacred vow from Joseph to be taken back and buried in the promised land.
20	Gen 48:1-22	Jacob blesses Joseph/DIVINE AFFIRMATION/Joseph is recognized for his integrity and receives fatherly blessing.
21	Gen 49:1-28	Jacob's final blessing to all/DIVINE AFFIRMATION/Joseph again well blessed.
22	Gen 49:29-50:3	Jacob's burial wish made public/SOVEREIGN GUIDANCE/The Hebrews must not lose sight of God's ultimate location for them.
23	Gen 50:4-12	Return for burial.
24	Gen 50:15-21	Joseph's brothers fear vengence/FINAL INTEGRITY CHECK, BENT OF LIFE/SENSE OF DESTINY/Joseph's character shines out.
25	Gen 50:22-26	Joseph's burial wish/FAITH/Joseph performs a final leadership act by giving a prophetical word of faith to his people. This word will bring great expectation and carry influence over the years to come.

VIGNETTES

Indirect Data

While there are many references in the Scripture to Joseph by name, the following add information to his leadership story. They are:

REFERENCE	INFORMATION
Psa 105:16-25	This shows the idea of the word check that Joseph was going through during his isolation time in Potiphar's home and the isolation in jail.
Heb 11:22	Points out the faith/prophetical aspect of Joseph's last leadership act: that of extracting a promise to have his remains buried in the promised land—don't forget that Jacob left him Shechem.
Josh 24:32	This shows the fulfillment of Joseph's faith/desire, his last leadership act for God's people.
Acts 7:9-15	This shows the impact of the sovereignty of God upon Joseph's entire life. This is a summary capsule of Joseph's life accomplishments and bent of life.
I Chron 5:2	This shows the importance of Joseph (and especially Judah) in the family line.

Birth Order Time-Line

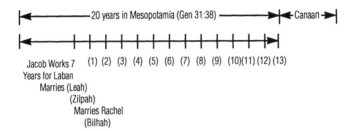

Leah's Own Children

1. Reuben
2. Simeon
3. Levi
4. Judah
9. Issachar
10. Zebulun
11. Dinah

Leah's Children Through Zilpah

7. Gad
8. Asher

Rachel's Children Through Bilhah

5. Dan
6. Naphtali

Rachel's Own Children

12. Joseph
13. Benjamin

Appendix C. Important Process Item Definitions

These definitions are taken from *Leadership Emergence Theory* by Dr. J. Robert Clinton. It is published by Barnabas Publishers P.O. Box 6006, Altadena, California, 91003-6006.

Process Items

Introduction   Previously, I defined leadership development as a life-time process in which God providentially works in developing a leader to operate at maximum potential—"according to the measure of faith" (Rom. 12:6). I said that the central concept for integrating the study was a time-line along the   horizontal axis. Along the vertical axis are categories of items which point out specific events, people, ways, etc. in which God operated in the selection process. These things listed along the vertical part of the leadership selection chart are process items.

Definition   ***Process items*** are those providential events, people, circumstances, special interventions, inner-life lessons, and/or anything which God uses in the leadership selection process of a person to:

> • indicate leadership potential (inner integrity, influence capacity),
> • develop (train) that potential,
> • confirm appointment to a role/responsibility,
> • move the leader along to God's appointed ministry level for the realized potential.

Examples
of General,
Common
Items

• sphere of influence
• contextual items
• spiritual authority
• crisis items
• power items
• family process items
• word checks

• obedience checks
• sovereign guidance
• spiritual gift-mix
• divine contacts
• literary influences
• isolation items
• leadership backlash

5 General Categories of Process Items

Introduction   It is often helpful to categorize, that is, organize process items. One such method is given below. The categories seem to follow a general ordering of categories as observed in numerous time line studies. The categorizing is not totally non-exclusive, that is, there is some overlap in categories and certain process items could fit under more than one category.

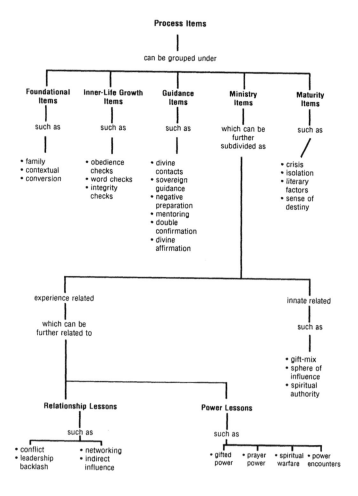

Integrity Check   syn. Inner-life check

Introduction	God often prepares a leader for a wider sphere of influence by testing the leader's integrity. Intent of the heart and follow through on intent are checked on an integrity check. Usually a successful passing of an integrity check results in a stronger leader able to serve God in a wider sphere of influence.
Definition	An ***integrity check*** refers to the special kind of process test which God uses to evaluate heart-intent and which God uses as a springboard to an expanded sphere of influence.
O.T. Example	Daniel (Dan 1,5); Shadrach, Meschach, and Abednego (Dan 3); Joseph (Gen 39); Abraham (Gen 24); Jephthah (Jud 11).
N.T. Example	Paul (Acts 20:22,23)

Kinds

- leadership backlash
- conflict against ministry vision
- alternative better offer in guidance situations
- temptation
- value check (ultimate value)
- prophecy of persecution
- word conflict or obedience conflict
- loyalty (who is first)

Uses

- to see follow-through in a promise or vow
- to insure burden for a ministry of vision
- to allow confirmation of inner-character strength
- to build faith
- to warn others of the seriousness of obeying God

Word Checks

Introduction   An essential characteristic of leadership is the ability to receive truth from God. This characteristic is essential to building spiritual authority which is the power base for a spiritual leader's influence. It is also an integral part of a leader's methodology for getting guidance for the ministry. Leaders greatly used of God have evidenced a love for truth. They study the written word to feed their own souls as well as to help those to whom they minister. They are quick to discern God's truth in every day life. They learn to hear the voice of God through the ministry of other people. So then, one would expect God to develop a leader in his/her ability to appreciate truth, to cultivate habits of intake of truth, and to obey truth. The process item used to describe this development is called the word process item. A special kind of word process item is a word check.

Definition   A *word check* is a process item which tests a leader's ability to appropriate God's truth and apply it to life and ministry.

Comment   When successfully passed a word check results in a leader increasing his/her ability to discern God's voice of truth, to clarify truth, and to apply it to life and ministry.

Example   Barnabas was sent to Antioch (Acts 11) to discern the genuineness of the reported gentile's turning to Christ. He had just been exposed to truth concerning God's acceptance of Cornelius. Now he will grow as he learns to apply that word to a new situation. Has he learned the truth? Is he willing to commit himself on the basis of that truth? Can he apply it to a new situation? This Ministry Task Process Item was informal training for Barnabas in developing his apostleship gift. One apostolic function is the ability to authoritatively use God's word to test genuineness of Christian expression.

Example   Peter was told by the Holy Spirit (Acts 10) to go with the three gentiles to Cornelius' home. This happened concurrently with the thrice repeated vision concerning clean and unclean. He immediately perceived new truth. The Gentiles were not unclean. He was then ready for the expansion of that truth which God gave at Cornelius' home. Peter was tested on two truths (Gentiles are clean and Jesus will baptize in the Holy Spirit).

Failure   Often failure to pass a word check results in repeated lessons and increased development time toward potential.

Divine Affirmation

Introduction   In a life time of ministry there will be times within a leader's ministry in which he/she will need the reassurance of God that the ministry is relevant and worthwhile and that the leader's life is indeed counting toward God's purposes. This reaffirmation is usually an inward need which will infuse new life to the leader. Occasionally, this affirmation is outward to confirm to followers that the leader does indeed have spiritual authority. The process item which described this special approval from God is called divine affirmation. It is closely linked with spiritual authority.

Definition   ***Divine affirmation*** is a special kind of sense of destiny experience in which God gives approval to a leader so that the leader has a renewed sense of ultimate purpose and a refreshed desire to continue serving God.

Comment   Usually the affirmation is an inward thing which satisfies the leader alone that God is indeed with him/her and that the life-purpose of serving God is real and vital and worthwhile. However, sometimes the affirmation is externally for others to know and see. The external divine affirmation usually is in connection with validation of spiritual authority.

Example   At least three times in Jesus ministry one can observe God's divine affirmation. See Mt 3:17, 17:5, Jn 12:27,28.

Example   From Gen 12:1-2 onward for more than 25 years God gave divine affirmation to Abraham periodically. See especially Gen 15 where God renewed Abraham's purpose and also revealed great truth.

Example   I Sam 12:13-19 is a great passage illustrating divine
                 affirmation of Samuel's ministry which is
                 primarily external.

Example   Acts 18:9,10 and 27:23-26 are divine affirmations
                 for Paul's ministry.

Forms of   Divine affirmation can come through:
Divine   • sovereign arrangement of circumstances,
Affirmation   • an inner voice or other direct revelation,
                       • a dream,
                       • a vision,
                       • angelic visitation,
                       • a prophetic word,
                       • a miraculous sign.

Convergence synonym: role match

Introduction   In the leadership emergence study of people who have had wide ministries and impact upon a large sphere of influence an often observed condition is convergence. Briefly stated convergence is the "coming together" of a number of factors including assignment of roles, experience, use of gifts, so that person can contribute toward the maximum potential for which God intended. In short, convergence refers to the "fit" of the right person for the right job at the right time.

Definition   ***Convergence*** refers to a ministry situation for a given person which maximizes the following factors so that the person ministers more efficiently and effectively.

CONVERGENCE FACTORS

Factor   Related to Convergence

Gift-mix   The person's gift mix is well identified, developed and has been   used in various ministry experiences <u>and</u> the person is increasingly choosing ministry priorities in terms of gift-mix and dominant gift.

Experience   The person's past experience (including development of gift-mix, lessons learned from major process items, variety of assignments, etc.) relate directly to the present ministry.

Temperament   The persons responsibility in terms of people relationships is ideally suited to the person's temperament and present emotional maturity.

Sphere of   The person's role and ministry responsibility
Influence   allow for the person to minister to the "sphere of

influence groups"best suited to the person's gift-mix and present development state.

Role   The formal role assigned not only frees the person from restrictions to use the gift-mix but actually enhances the use of gift-mix.

Biblical   Jephthah, the 9th Judge (charismatic crisis leader)
Example   is an old testament example of convergence. His third development phase in which he delivers Israel (those in Gilead and Manasseh) from the Ammonites demonstrates convergence. Role, experience and natural abilities all converge in this third phase. Role and experience are especially prominent. Giftedness is less seen but is implicit.

Sense of Destiny syn: divine intervention

Introduction   God often intervenes in the lives of leaders who will eventually rise to types D (rational) and E (intentional) in such a way as to inspire them to attempt great things for Him.   These special unique interventions are touched with the sense of the mystical. This special kind of process item is   called "sense of destiny."

Definition   A *sense of destiny* process item is a unique awe-inspiring experience
   • in which God reveals Himself,
   • to an obedient surrendered believer,
   • in order to inspire/lead that person on to accomplish something special in his/her life-time.

Examples   Abraham: Gen 12:-1-3; 13:14,15; 15:1ff; 17:1; 18:1 (inner heart voice, audible voice, vision, Angelic visitor) Joseph: Gen 37:5 dream; 37:9 dream; 45:5 fulfillment Moses: Ex 2:8 divine intervention "Take this child..." Ex 3:2 supernatural phenomena (burning bush) Jephthah: Judges 10,11 (crisis identity) Daniel (many—in word, vision, angelic beings) Paul Acts 9; 22; 26 see especially Acts 26:15ff vs 19. "I did not disobey the vision."

Summary: audible voice, deep conviction in the heart, dreams, visions, unusual occurrence in nature, word.

Others observed   surrender experience, prophetic utterance, integrity check, divine contacts,   mystical presence of Christ, divine confirmation experiences.

Comment   Often related to a "call experience" but also related to "keeping on target confirmation experiences."

4 Principles   1. It Is The Living Eternal Almighty God Who Gives A "Sense Of Destiny." He can do anything He pleases. Note that names of God in the Old Testament often come with a sense of destiny experience. We know God more deeply after a sense of destiny experience.

                 2. God Looks For One Who Is Willing To Be Obedient and Used For God's Purposes - To That Kind Comes A Sense of Destiny . Not all will have this.

                 3. The Sense Of Destiny Experience May Be Repeated More Than Once In A Lifetime. Usually awe-inspiring and not easily forgotten. Sometimes it is mystifying and only seen later after time has passed. Some reasons for repeated sense of destiny experiences.

                     A. To affirm/confirm that we are still going to be used.

                     B. To help our sagging faith.

                     C. To clarify further, to reveal intermediate steps.

                 4. When God Chooses You For His Purposes Be Obedient And Believe That He Will Accomplish That Destiny Through You.

Four Marks of a Sense of Destiny
Four Suggestions Concerning a Sense of Destiny

Introduction   It is helpful to know some of the items that can help one identify sense of destiny experiences. The following are some suggestions toward that end.

Four marks   When you have a "sense of destiny" experience (at least when you become aware that it was such an experience),

1. You know experientially that the living God has touched you.

2. You believe He has something worthwhile for you to accomplish in your life-time,

3. You obediently follow along as God carries you on to the accomplishment of that destiny. He will do what He promises.

4. At the end of your life-time you can rejoice in knowing your *life counted* in the purposes of God.

Four Suggestions

Remember   In its essence, a sense of destiny is a deep inner recognition that God is going to use you as an integral part of his purposes whether in a small role or large role. It is that sense of God being in it and the importance of it that makes a sense of destiny experience vital. Ask God to give you a sense of destiny no matter the "size" of work you are in or your "giftedness."

Suggestion 1   Seek To Confirm That *Inner Call* That What You Are Doing Is Right On Target And Important To God's Purposes For You and His Work. (When it is all said and done you want to know that what you have given your life for has counted.)

Suggestion 2   Make Your Major Decisions Based On:
· your sense of destiny,
· your gift/mix,
· your role matched to gift-mix,

Suggestion 3   Expect God To Repeatedly Confirm Your Sense of Destiny As He Moves You On To Your Maximum Potential For Your Sphere Of Influence.

Suggestion 4   Concentrate On Those Things Which Build Spiritual Authority.

· word,
· life,
· prayer power,
· power

And Leave Promotion Along The Sphere Of Influence To God.

Bent of Life

Introduction   When doing studies involving Historical Biographies one is tempted to continually ask such questions as, "Is this true? Is this the way it really happened? Are they trying to paint this character too pretty?" There is that tendency to criticize. One must be careful to realize that you are not seeing the data but someone's reflection of it. You are seeing the character through someone else's perspective. So there is that continual attempt to validate and perhaps read the material critically. Now validation, while normal, is not always the most productive way to look at the "filtered data." A more useful way to look at the data is not to say is this true, but to say if it were true does it give perspectives that are helpful? If the perspectives in themselves are helpful they in one sense then are true. When reading the New Testament appraisal of Old Testament characters such as Abraham and David and the heroes of faith you will note that the reports do not tell the whole story, instead they highlight the major trend or heart intent or purpose of God accomplished in the life. This "bent of life" appraisal is what is sought in doing leadership studies. While criticism has its place leadership studies are not primarily critical but are "heuristic" in nature and are seeking to discover the helpful leadership principles that can be drawn from the "perceived data."

Definition   ***Bent of life*** refers to the analysis of a character for the most productive findings of that character's life and ministry.

Example   When the Bible analyzes Abraham's walk with God
                   in Rom 4 (see Abraham especially verses 20, 21)
                   it points out the trend or heart intent of
                   Abraham to believe God. An examination of the
                   record in Genesis will show that there were
                   several times when that faith faltered. But the
                   heart intent, the bent of life, of Abraham was to
                   believe God as described in verses 20,21. And it
                   is that positive aspect of Abraham's walk that is
                   highlighted and used to point out truth for others.
                   This same "bent of life" approach is used when
                   James evaluates Abraham's faith in James 2:18-24.

Example   Keith Hinton (OMF missionary in Singapore) did
                   an in-depth leadership study of David. His analysis
                   shows that the latter development phases for
                   David were down hill. However, the testimony
                   given David in Acts 13:36 (...for David, after he
                   had served his own generation by the will of
                   God...) was bent of life.

Guideline   When reading biographies of characters, seek to
                   put the very best construction on the
                   interpretations of the author. Rather than critically
                   viewing and having a negative bias, seek to identify
                   principles, leadership lessons, and guidelines from
                   the writing as though it were absolutely true. The
                   purpose of a leadership study is to learn and profit
                   from the study.

Development   It is this "bent of life" approach that you are seeking
Phase Label   to capture when you identify and label a
                   development phase.